THERE'S A TREASURE AWAITS INSIDE

Inspired by Jon Collins-Black

Gloria o. Sarah

5 FAQs about "There's Treasure Inside"

What is "There's Treasure Inside"?

- "There's Treasure Inside" is a real-world treasure hunt book written by Jon Collins-Black. It contains a series of clues and puzzles that lead to a hidden treasure.

Is the treasure real?

- Yes, the treasure is real and is worth millions of dollars.
- How can I participate in the treasure hunt?

To participate, you need to purchase the book "There's Treasure Inside" and start solving the clues and puzzles presented within it.

Is there an online community for "There's Treasure Inside"?

- Yes, there is a vibrant online community of "Seekers" who discuss theories, share clues, and collaborate to solve the puzzles.

What are the ethical considerations of treasure hunting?

- Treasure hunting should be done responsibly and ethically, respecting private property, historical sites, and the environment. It's crucial to obtain necessary permissions and avoid damaging cultural heritage.

TABLE OF CONTENT

historical references, and real-world implications have sparked countless hours of discussion, debate, and problem-solving. It has inspired people to think critically, explore creatively, and embrace the thrill of the unknown.

A Legacy of Adventure

Whether or not the treasure is ever found, "There's Treasure Inside" has already left a lasting legacy. It has inspired countless people to embark on their own adventures, big and small. It has shown us the power of community, collaboration, and the enduring appeal of a good mystery. And it has reminded us that sometimes, the greatest treasure of all is the journey itself.

Author's background and connection to treasure hunting

Jon Collins-Black, the mastermind behind *"There's Treasure Inside,"* is a fascinating figure who has captivated the attention of treasure hunters and puzzle enthusiasts worldwide. His background and connection to treasure hunting are as intriguing as the hunt itself.

A Passion for Puzzles and Adventure

Jon Collins-Black has always had a passion for puzzles and problem-solving. As a child, he was drawn to riddles, codes, and mysteries. This early interest sparked a lifelong fascination with the thrill of the chase and the satisfaction of uncovering hidden truths.

The Birth of a Treasure Hunter

Collins-Black's journey into the world of treasure hunting began in his early adulthood. He was captivated by the stories of legendary treasure hunts, such as the search for the lost city of El Dorado or the pirate treasure of Captain Kidd. These tales of adventure and riches ignited a spark within him, prompting him to embark on his own treasure-hunting expeditions.

puzzles, and support one another on their quest. This collaborative spirit fosters a sense of camaraderie and excitement, as participants work together to unravel the mysteries of the book. The online community has become an integral part of the treasure hunt, enhancing the overall experience for all involved.

A Testament to Human Ingenuity

"There's Treasure Inside" is a testament to the power of human imagination and ingenuity. The intricate puzzles, historical references, and real-world implications have sparked countless hours of discussion, debate, and problem-solving. It has inspired people to think critically, explore creatively, and embrace the thrill of the unknown. The book's ability to captivate and engage its audience is a testament to its unique blend of real-world adventure, historical intrigue, and mind-bending puzzles.

A Legacy of Adventure

Whether or not the treasure is ever found, "There's Treasure Inside" has already left a lasting legacy. It has inspired countless people to embark on their own adventures, big and small. It has shown us the power of community, collaboration, and the enduring appeal of a good mystery. And it has reminded us that sometimes, the greatest treasure of all is the journey itself.

A treasure trove of possibilities

The treasure hidden within the pages of *"There's Treasure Inside"* is as diverse and intriguing as the clues that lead to it. This eclectic collection of artifacts and valuables reflects the boundless imagination and creativity of its creator, Jon Collins-Black. By curating such a varied assortment of treasures, Collins-Black has ensured that there is something to captivate everyone, from history buffs to pop culture enthusiasts.

A Blend of the Old and the New

One of the most striking aspects of the treasure is its blend of historical artifacts and contemporary treasures. The collection includes items that span centuries, from ancient coins and relics to modern collectibles and digital assets. This juxtaposition of the old and the new creates a fascinating contrast and highlights the enduring appeal of treasure hunting across different eras.

Historical Artifacts and Cultural Significance

A significant portion of the treasure consists of historical artifacts that offer a glimpse into the past. These items may include:

- o Ancient Coins and Relics: These objects can provide insights into ancient civilizations, their economies, and their cultural practices.
- o Art and Collectibles: The treasure may contain rare and valuable works of art, such as paintings, sculptures, or decorative objects.
- o Historical Documents: Original documents, letters, or manuscripts can shed light on important historical events and figures.

- Artistic Symbolism: The use of artistic symbols, such as alchemical symbols or religious iconography, can add layers of meaning to the clues.

The Role of Collaboration

The complexity of the puzzles in *"There's Treasure Inside"* often necessitates collaboration. By sharing ideas, knowledge, and resources, readers can collectively overcome challenges and make significant progress. Online forums and social media groups have emerged as important platforms for collaboration, allowing participants to connect with like-minded individuals and work together to solve the puzzles.

The Thrill of the Chase

The process of deciphering the clues and solving the puzzles is as rewarding as the ultimate goal of finding the treasure. The feeling of accomplishment that comes with cracking a difficult code or uncovering a hidden meaning is exhilarating. This sense of achievement drives readers to continue their quest, even in the face of setbacks and frustrations.

- Historical Documents: Original documents, letters, and manuscripts can shed light on important historical events, political figures, and social movements. They can also reveal personal stories and intimate details about the lives of individuals.
- Art and Collectibles: Historical art and collectibles can offer a glimpse into the aesthetic sensibilities of past cultures. They can also reveal information about the social and economic status of their owners.

Personal Connections and Family Legacies

Many of the artifacts within the treasure may have personal connections to the individuals who owned them. These objects can be passed down through generations, carrying with them family histories, cultural traditions, and emotional significance. By understanding the stories behind these objects, we can appreciate their value beyond their monetary worth.

- Family Heirlooms: Heirlooms can represent family history, cultural identity, and personal memories. They can be passed down from generation to generation, carrying with them the stories and traditions of a family.
- Personal Collections: Objects collected by individuals can reflect their passions, interests, and experiences. They can

provide insights into their personalities, their travels, and their relationships with others.

The Intrigue of the Unknown

The mystery surrounding the origins and histories of some of the artifacts adds to their allure. As participants in the treasure hunt delve deeper into the clues and puzzles, they may uncover surprising stories and unexpected connections. The process of uncovering these hidden narratives is a rewarding experience that can spark curiosity and imagination.

The Cultural Impact

"There's Treasure Inside" has not only captivated individuals but has also had a significant cultural impact, sparking conversations, inspiring creativity, and fostering a sense of community. This treasure hunt has transcended its original purpose, becoming a cultural phenomenon that has resonated with people from all walks of life.

A Modern-Day Myth

The treasure hunt has taken on a mythical quality, inspiring stories and legends. It has become a subject of speculation, with countless theories and interpretations circulating online. This collective storytelling has

THE PSYCHOLOGICAL AND SOCIAL ASPECTS

The Psychology of the Hunt

The allure of treasure hunting extends far beyond the promise of material wealth. It taps into a deep-seated human desire for adventure, discovery, and the thrill of the chase. By understanding the psychological motivations and emotions that drive treasure hunters, we can gain insight into the enduring appeal of this ancient pursuit.

The Thrill of the Chase

At the heart of treasure hunting lies the thrill of the chase. The anticipation of discovering something valuable, the excitement of solving a complex puzzle, and the satisfaction of overcoming challenges all contribute to a sense of exhilaration. This psychological reward system is deeply ingrained in human nature, driving us to seek out new experiences and conquer obstacles.

The Desire for Adventure

Treasure hunting offers an opportunity to escape the mundane and embark on an adventure. The prospect of exploring new places, encountering unexpected challenges, and pushing the boundaries of one's comfort zone is a powerful motivator. This desire for adventure is often linked to a longing for freedom, independence, and a sense of self-discovery.

The Quest for Meaning

For many treasure hunters, the search for hidden treasure is a quest for meaning. It is an opportunity to connect with history, to understand the past, and to leave a lasting legacy. The discovery of a historical artifact or a personal treasure can provide a sense of purpose and fulfillment.

The Social Aspect

Treasure hunting can be a social activity, bringing people together to collaborate and share experiences. The camaraderie and shared sense of purpose can create strong bonds and lasting friendships. Social interaction and the feeling of belonging are important human needs, and treasure hunting can provide a satisfying outlet for these needs.

can damage archaeological sites and destroy valuable historical information.

Environmental Impact

- ○ Minimal Impact: Treasure hunters should strive to minimize their impact on the environment. This includes avoiding littering, respecting wildlife habitats, and avoiding damage to natural features.
- ○ Sustainable Practices: When exploring remote areas, it is important to practice Leave No Trace principles. This means packing out all trash, minimizing campfires, and avoiding damage to vegetation.

Respect for Private Property

- ○ Obtain Permission: Treasure hunters should always obtain permission from landowners before exploring private property. Trespassing can lead to legal consequences and damage relationships with landowners.
- ○ Avoid Intrusion: Even on public lands, it is important to respect the privacy of others. Avoid disturbing wildlife, damaging fences, or trespassing on private property.

Cultural Sensitivity

- o Respect Local Customs: When exploring areas with cultural significance, treasure hunters should be respectful of local customs and traditions. This includes avoiding disturbing sacred sites or cultural artifacts.
- o Sensitivity to Indigenous Peoples: If exploring areas with indigenous populations, it is important to be sensitive to their cultural practices and beliefs. Avoid disturbing sacred sites or interfering with traditional customs.

Ethical Collecting

- o Legal Acquisition: All artifacts and treasures should be acquired legally. This means obtaining permits, licenses, or other necessary authorizations.
- o Responsible Ownership: Once acquired, artifacts should be cared for properly and protected from damage or theft.
- o Ethical Disposal: If an artifact is not of significant historical or cultural value, it should be disposed of responsibly, such as donating it to a museum or historical society.

Cultural Sensitivity

- ○ Respect Local Customs: When exploring areas with cultural significance, treasure hunters should be respectful of local customs and traditions. This includes avoiding disturbing sacred sites or cultural artifacts.
- ○ Sensitivity to Indigenous Peoples: If exploring areas with indigenous populations, it is important to be sensitive to their cultural practices and beliefs. Avoid disturbing sacred sites or interfering with traditional customs.

Ethical Collecting

- ○ Legal Acquisition: All artifacts and treasures should be acquired legally. This means obtaining permits, licenses, or other necessary authorizations.
- ○ Responsible Ownership: Once acquired, artifacts should be cared for properly and protected from damage or theft.
- ○ Ethical Disposal: If an artifact is not of significant historical or cultural value, it should be disposed of responsibly, such as donating it to a museum or historical society.

The Role of the Online Community

- ○ The online community of treasure hunters can play a significant role in promoting ethical behavior. By sharing best practices, encouraging responsible exploration, and discouraging unethical behavior, the community can help to ensure that treasure hunting remains a positive and sustainable activity.

A Comparison to Other Treasure Hunts

"There's Treasure Inside" stands out among other famous treasure hunts due to its unique blend of historical intrigue, complex puzzles, and a strong online community. Let's compare it to some of the most iconic treasure hunts in history.

The Fenn Treasure

One of the most recent and well-known treasure hunts is the Fenn Treasure. Hidden by Forrest Fenn, a renowned art dealer, the treasure was described in Fenn's memoir, "The Thrill of the Chase." The Fenn Treasure, like "There's Treasure Inside," relied on cryptic clues and poetic riddles to guide seekers to the hidden cache. However, unlike "There's Treasure Inside," the Fenn Treasure was a more traditional treasure hunt, relying on physical exploration and outdoor skills.

The Oak Island Mystery

The Oak Island Mystery is a centuries-old treasure hunt centered around Oak Island in Nova Scotia, Canada. Numerous attempts have been

Ethical Considerations and Legal Frameworks

- o Preservation of Cultural Heritage: As treasure hunting becomes more popular, it is essential to balance the thrill of the chase with the preservation of cultural heritage. Strict regulations may be imposed to protect historical sites and artifacts.

- o Environmental Protection: Treasure hunting activities should be conducted in a way that minimizes environmental impact. Strict regulations may be imposed to protect sensitive ecosystems and natural resources.

- o Data Privacy and Security: As technology plays a larger role in treasure hunting, it is important to address concerns related to data privacy and security. Strong measures must be taken to protect personal information and prevent cyber-attacks.

The Future of Treasure Hunting

As technology continues to evolve, we can expect to see even more innovative and exciting treasure hunts in the future. Virtual reality, augmented reality, and artificial intelligence could be used to create immersive and interactive experiences. However, it is essential to ensure that these advancements are used responsibly and ethically.

The future of treasure hunting will depend on our ability to balance the thrill of the chase with the preservation of cultural heritage and the environment. By embracing the spirit of adventure while respecting the past, we can ensure that treasure hunting remains a rewarding and sustainable hobby for generations to come.

Embark on Your Own Adventure

Inspired by the thrilling journey of "There's Treasure Inside," why not embark on your own adventure? Whether it's a physical exploration or an intellectual pursuit, the world is full of mysteries waiting to be uncovered.

Physical Adventures:

- o Geocaching: A global treasure hunt that uses GPS devices to find hidden containers.
- o Hiking and Camping: Explore the great outdoors and discover hidden gems in nature.
- o Travel: Visit new places, immerse yourself in different cultures, and experience the world firsthand.

Intellectual Adventures:

- o Puzzle Solving: Engage your mind with puzzles, riddles, and codes.
- o Coding and Programming: Learn to create your own digital worlds and solve complex problems.
- o Writing and Storytelling: Craft your own narratives and share your unique perspective with the world.

PERSONAL NOTES